THE UNIVERSE AND YOU

Written by
Suzanne Slade

Illustrated by
Stephanie Fizer Coleman

PUBLISHED BY SLEEPING BEAR PRESS

Daylight dims.

Darkness tiptoes in.

You're tucked in tight
for a warm, cozy **night**.

The **earth** beneath you
seems solid.
Still.

But gently,

ever so gently,

it **spins,**

lulling you to sleep.

And while you sleep,
our beautiful blue **Earth**
and seven other **planets**

circle the **sun**

Earth

Mercury

Venus

Uranus

Neptune

Jupiter

Saturn

Mars

in our **solar system.**

Earth **orbits** the sun
around and around,

carrying majestic mountains,

bellowing bullfrogs,

delicate daisies,

and **you**!
Silently snoozing you.

And while you sleep,
dreaming big dreams,

our fiery sun

and billions of other bright **stars**

swirl and whirl

around our gorgeous **galaxy**—

the **Milky Way**.

And while you still sleep,
dreaming even bigger dreams,

billions of galaxies,

each with their own swirling, whirling stars,

slowly slide away from each other

in the **ever-expanding**

expanse of **space**—

our universe!

And then,
in the blink of an eye—
it happens!

Right on cue

our glorious sun

peeks above Earth's **horizon**.

to sparkling streams,

towering trees,

hungry hummingbirds,

and *you*!
Silently stirring you.

And when you wake,

all the **galaxies** in the **universe**,

all the **stars** in the **Milky Way**,

all the **planets** in the **solar system**

are still moving,
circling,
and swirling.

Darkness is gone.

Daylight has dawned.

And you're ready to play
on this brand-new **day!**

Earth looks like a brilliant blue ball (with a few white clouds overhead) because nearly three-fourths of its surface is covered with water. Credit: NASA

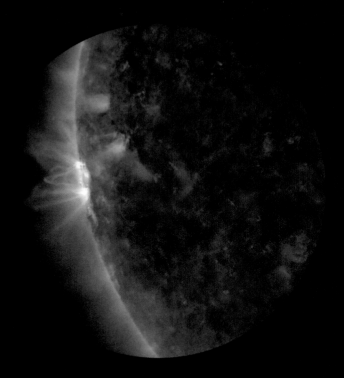

The sizzling surface of the sun reaches 9,941 degrees Fahrenheit (5,505 degrees Celsius!). The sun is so massive that more than one million Earths could fit inside it. Credit: NASA/GSFC/Solar Dynamics Observatory

Exploring the Universe

Earth is always on the move! It spins around an imaginary line through its center called an axis, and makes one complete rotation in 24 hours. That's why a day lasts 24 hours.

Earth orbits, or circles, the sun, along with seven other planets—Mercury, Venus, Mars, Jupiter, Saturn, Uranus, and Neptune. They are part of our solar system (which also contains dwarf planets, moons, and other small celestial bodies). The sun's large mass creates a powerful force called gravity, which holds the solar system together.

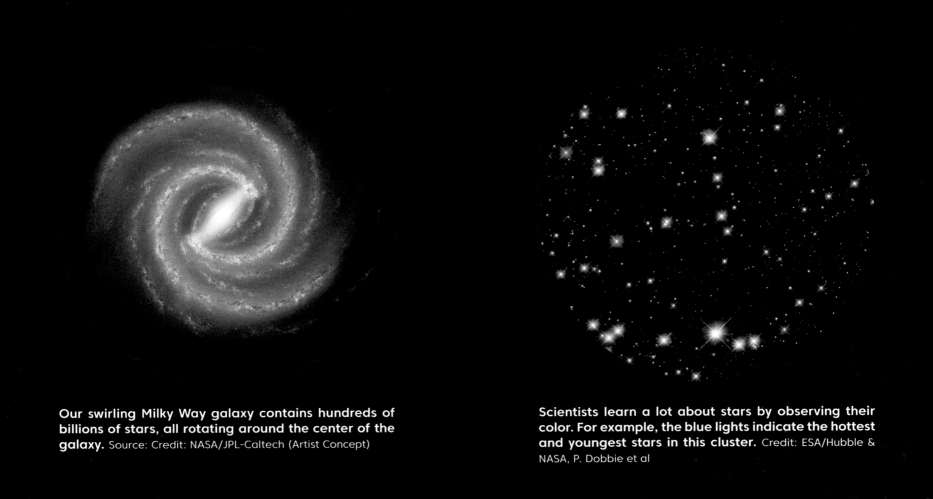

Our swirling Milky Way galaxy contains hundreds of billions of stars, all rotating around the center of the galaxy. Source: Credit: NASA/JPL-Caltech (Artist Concept)

Scientists learn a lot about stars by observing their color. For example, the blue lights indicate the hottest and youngest stars in this cluster. Credit: ESA/Hubble & NASA, P. Dobbie et al

Our solar system is part of the Milky Way galaxy, which holds more than 100 billion stars. It's hard to imagine something that huge.

But our universe is much bigger! It's so massive, scientists aren't sure how many galaxies it contains, but they think it's at least hundreds of billions. Our vast universe includes everything! All people, animals, and plants. All planets, stars, and galaxies. The universe even contains space, light, and time. It's the largest thing that exists. And scientists say the universe is still expanding and growing bigger all the time!

To Delia, whose generous spirit shines like a brilliant star

—Suzanne

★

For Seth, always

—Stephanie

SLEEPING BEAR PRESS™
2395 South Huron Parkway, Suite 200
Ann Arbor, MI 48104
www.sleepingbearpress.com

Printed and bound in the United States.

10 9 8 7 6 5 4 3 2 1

Library of Congress Cataloging-in-Publication Data

Names: Slade, Suzanne, author. | Coleman, Stephanie Fizer, illustrator.
Title: The universe and you / written by Suzanne Slade ;
illustrated by Stephanie Fizer Coleman.
Description: Ann Arbor, MI : Sleeping Bear Press, [2021] | Audience: Ages
4-8 | Summary: "During the night, as a child sleeps in her bedroom, the
reader is taken on an exploration of our solar system, galaxies beyond,
and finally the universe as a whole"– Provided by publisher.
Identifiers: LCCN 2021005303 | ISBN 9781534111080 (hardcover)
Subjects: LCSH: Astronomy—Juvenile literature. | Sleep—Juvenile literature.
Classification: LCC QB46 .S583 2021 | DDC 523—dc23
LC record available at https://lccn.loc.gov/2021005303